I AM

10 Things God Says About Me

Jose Gonzalez

Copyright © 2020 Jose Gonzalez

ISBN: 978-1-64718-622-7

Library of Congress Cataloging in Publication Data
Gonzalez, Jose
I AM: 10 Things God Says About Me by Jose Gonzalez
Library of Congress Control Number: 2020909824

Published by BookLocker.com, Inc., St. Petersburg, Florida.

Printed on acid-free paper.

BookLocker.com, Inc.
2020

Scripture quotations marked (NLT) are taken from the Holy Bible, New Living Translation, copyright ©1996, 2004, 2015 by Tyndale House Foundation. Used by permission of Tyndale House Publishers, a Division of Tyndale House Ministries, Carol Stream, Illinois 60188. All rights reserved.

Scriptures taken from the Holy Bible, New International Version®, NIV®. Copyright © 1973, 1978, 1984, 2011 by Biblica, Inc.™ Used by

I dedicate this book first and foremost to the lover of my soul, thank You for loving me so much that even when I was yet a sinner, You died for me. Next, to my family and friends (too many to name individually) whom I love so very dearly. I may not have always been or will be the greatest reflection of Christ and for that I am sorry, yet it is my prayer that as you read this your faith and understanding about who Jesus is will grow as you learn. Finally, I would like to thank everyone who supported me during the adventure of writing this book, for without your support and longing to see the finished project I probably would have given up.

Table of Contents

Prologue

I'd like to welcome you to take this journey with the countless others who will be reading this book. I set out to write this book because I am a people watcher, not to judge but because I genuinely love the human creation with all its triumphs, inventions, faults, feelings, and even failures. All these years of watching people, I noticed that there are too many people who don't know who they are.

I observed that there is a severe case of identity crisis in the world and, more importantly, in the Church, and because they don't know who they are, they are prone to a life that comes short of the abundant life of which Jesus spoke. I'm sure various studies can prove my observation, but if you want those facts and figures, this is not the book for you. One of the few questions I noticed that people have been asking over the past few years has been "Who am I?", What is my purpose?" "What do I want?" "Why am I rarely satisfied?" or "Why can't people see the real me beyond my skin color, job or financial status?" I believe that we as humans tend to ask these questions because we were created for a purpose, and that purpose, in my opinion, is that we were created to be free to be the people that our God, Creator, and Father designed us to be.

Walking according to who God says I am is important to me because I come from a culture that often dictated what you were and dictated what you should be doing in life. No longer am I bound by that. Now, for me, it's just about being. Seeing myself as God sees me is my ultimate goal, and I hope you also make that your goal.

In my early times with the Word of the Lord, I believed that it was all about the God who stated: "I Will" like in passages found in Jeremiah 31:33-34. I believed with my entire heart that it was about The Father who did it for us because we could not do it for ourselves. Then, unfortunately, my beliefs came under fire. The Church I began to attend had weak teaching in this area; they were teaching that our faith is all about doing rather than being and relying on what God says He did. What did I know? I was a kid off the streets. Me, compete with these seasoned church folks? Now, let me get this straight. I didn't think it was a competition, I thought we were family, but they thought I should just shut up and obey what they were teaching. The problem I had with that that line of thinking was that it conflicted with what I was reading in my Bible.

Due to my experiences and lack of active teaching from the leaders I was following, I fell into a mixture of beliefs. This is where my identity crisis began. I started believing that my faith was based on what I did and not solely based on what God said. I must tell you as I look back, it caused a lot of pain and confusion in my life. It saddens me to acknowledge that due to my thinking I was even guilty of ostracizing unbelievers. To them, if you are reading, please, forgive me.

We will be getting into the meat of the book shortly, but first, allow me to share a little insight into the beginning of my testimony. I want to share this because maybe you will see the God who initially revealed Himself to me and how grateful I am that He did. Some people can tell you the exact date they were saved. I am not one of those people. All I can say is that I was 19, and that my friends, was many years ago.

It was a scorching summer day in Buffalo, New York. We don't get many of those, so that sticks out in my mind. I remember riding my bike home from a female friend's house, who I used to smoke marijuana and have sex with. I remember finally getting home drenched from my ride, high and thinking I was going to die from heat stroke. No one was home and I distinctly remember wanting to shower and go straight to my room because I had an air conditioner in there. After being in that grueling heat, there was no place I wanted to be more than in my room. We lived in a two-floor split level townhouse, and at the top of the stairs, there was a light brown bookshelf that was about 3ft high and contained various books. One thing about this bookshelf that sticks out in my memory is that it was never orderly. That day as I reached the top of the staircase one book caught my attention in the midst of the many others. It was a Bible. Sitting on top of the bookshelf was a green leather King James Bible, and for some reason, I picked it up. Allow me to remind you I'm still high at this point. I remember saying to myself, "I'm going to read this for myself, and I know how this works, I'm going to open it and bam! It's going to speak directly to me" What was I thinking? My life has never been the same since.

Before I continue, let me explain a little about my family's history and experience with the faith. I spent my early childhood years with my grandmother, who was a Catholic. I remember going to Midnight mass on the holidays, her praying the rosary, the iconic artwork, the "Stations of the cross" in the Church, the Easter parade where we got to see a reenactment of Jesus carrying the cross, and her Bible. You see, my grandmother didn't know how to read, yet I remember her Bible because it was sort of enshrined in her living room. My grandmother's Bible was covered in plastic, and it could not be touched because it was the holiest thing in the house.

Fast forward several years to living with my mother who at one point was married to a South African man whose family were Christian ministers. To say my religious experience was vastly different from what I had when I lived with my grandmother would be an understatement. One was very quiet and the other was extremely loud. I was dragged to Church services that lasted for what seemed like an eternity. At that point in my life I just wanted to go outside and play. Having to endure Church felt like torture to me. The music always seemed to be so loud. They were always praying, so much so that it was even done before people traveled. Our house seemed to be a midpoint for people who were continually passing through on their way to the various church events they would be attending. I didn't understand it all but what I did know is that I didn't want to be there doing all the things these people were doing.

Because of my various experiences with Church, I never really questioned the reality of God. I just didn't believe that God was intimate and personal. At that point in my life, I would have to say that I was more agnostic, if anything.

So back to my story... I just finished riding a bike in what felt like a million degrees, I'm hot, sweaty, and I know that I was aggravated since I hate to be hot. I have the Bible in hand, and I open it believing that it would work like I would imagine magic does, and read a passage about "seeing the Lord in the land of the living" instantly I closed the Bible not even taking note where it was that I read the passage. I closed the Bible quickly because I was immediately under self-condemnation by what I read. I didn't think I was a bad person by any stretch or means; I just knew that my life was not right and that I didn't qualify to see the Lord in the land of the living. What did I do? I'm glad you asked. I said to myself, "lemme try this again I know for sure the Bible is going to talk to me for real this time" So there I went, I just opened it to a random page knowing God is going to talk to me. If this were a text message, I'd be using the emoji with the dashes as eyes right now, or a face palm. What was I thinking of trying this again after seeing what I read the first time? So, I opened it up again, and there I was ninety-nine percent scared and one percent curious. What do I see? You sure you want to know? Well ... keep reading. "Thus saith the LORD, Set thine house in order, for thou shall die, and not live" 2 Kings 20:1.

Yea, I know what you are thinking, trust me; I was thinking the same exact thing. "Why did I pick up this book?" At that point, my high was blown, but this time I didn't stop reading. I remember going to my room without showering and reading about a king who, like me, didn't think he was an overly bad guy yet to God that didn't matter. All that mattered was His word to the king.

You can find the story of King Hezekiah starting in 2 Kings 20, and I encourage that you read it for yourself. I won't tell you how the story ends, but I'll let you know what I found and didn't find that day. I didn't find a God who was far away and distant, but rather One who cared about His creation. I didn't encounter a God who wanted to judge me but instead longed to be merciful. I was embraced by a loving, close God who wanted to be my Father and wanted me to know Him for myself by understanding what He says both about Himself and me.

From that moment on, I loved to read His Word. I wanted to know more about this God. I would lock myself in my room and read for hours. Hours turned into days, days into weeks, weeks into months, and months into years. It's been many years since that time, and while some of my convictions may have changed, my Heavenly Father has not.

I have been to, and part of several churches since I began my journey as a Christian. I can honestly say I have even gotten kicked out of a church before, but that is not what defines me. What defines me is not what I do or don't do but rather who and what God says I am. I am grateful to say that I know who I am, and I continue to learn more every day. Having a better understanding of who you are in Christ is vital because when you know who you are and where you stand in God's eyes, then and only then can the real you rise from the noise of the world and shine to be who He created you to be.

Now, I know that this book might ruffle a few feathers, but that is not my intent. I intend to provide scripture-based evidence about who we are in hopes that your faith would grow because of what God says, rather than what I say. This resource I created for the body of Christ is by no way shape or form exhaustive. I am presenting only ten designations of who we are in Christ as a basis, a bedrock if you will, on which you can build your faith.

Whose Voice?

"The voice of the LORD is powerful, The voice
of the LORD is majestic."
Psalm 29:4 NASB

There is no greater joy I remember having than when someone believed me. It could have been me telling an absurd story to my younger siblings and them believing it with wonder in their eyes or me being believed when I was actually telling the truth. There was nothing like it.

I am sure that if you would ask many people, both believers, and unbelievers, what the first sin was they would say when Adam and Eve ate the apple or fruit or knowledge of good and evil. While that wouldn't be 100% incorrect, I would submit that the actual sin occurred before that event. I would submit to you that the fall happened because Man listened to the wrong voice. You might be asking what this has to do with our identity? I propose to you that knowing who you are from the One who made you has everything to do with your identity. Who better knows the creation than the very creator Himself? God says, "Before I formed you in the womb I knew you" Jeremiah 1:5a (New American Standard Bible). God knew who we would be, what we would like, all our quirks, all of our dislikes and pet peeves. He knew what would make us tick and who we are. Wouldn't you want to listen to the one who made us and knows us so intimately that He formed us?

We have to go all the way back to the fall of man to see what happened. In Genesis 2:16-17 (NASB) You will find an account of God saying to Adam "From any tree in the Garden you may eat freely; but from the tree of knowledge of good and evil you shall not eat, for in the day that you eat from it you will surely die" Go forward a few short verses. We find the conversation that the serpent had with Eve recorded for us illustrating how important it is to believe the correct voice. In Genesis 3:1-4, the following occurred: "Now the serpent was craftier than any beast of the field which the LORD God had made. And he said to the woman, "Indeed, has God said, 'You shall not eat from any tree of the garden'?" The woman said to the serpent, "From the fruit of the trees of the garden we may eat; but from the fruit of the tree which is in the middle of the garden, God has said, 'You shall not eat from it or touch it, or you will die.'" The serpent said to the woman, "You surely will not die!" Do you see what happened here? The serpent got Eve to question what voice it was that they should listen to, and as history has shown us, they made the wrong decision.

In the following chapters, you will find what God says about those who are in Christ. If God said it, who are we to not believe it? The reason that He gave us His Word is so that we could know what it is that He says about Himself and us. The more we read what He says and the more we take Him at His Word, the more secure we will be in who we are. I know that our life doesn't always reflect what His Word says, but I would say that it takes more faith to believe what God says about me even though I don't see it yet, and what is this thing about if it's not about faith?

So, I challenge you, to whose words are you going to listen? Are you going to listen to the world? Yourself? Your friends? Your family? Your experiences? Real news? Fake news? Whatever other things that are trying to influence you, or are you going to listen to the God who loves you so much that "He gave His only begotten son that who so ever believes in Him shall not perish but have eternal life" John 3:16. I challenge you to choose to believe the Father who loves you and challenge you to read all the verses I reference so that you would know for yourself that you see it in His Word, and no one will ever be able to take that away from you.

Prayer

Father, I thank You for Your Word. I thank You that every Word that proceeds from Your mouth will not return void. I thank You that You are the God who loves us so much that You would speak to us and give us Your living Word and Your Son. I thank You that You are a good Father. Help me to believe what You say, no matter if I see it right away in my life or not. I put my faith in You and what you say. I trust what You say about me and what You say about You. In Jesus' name, I pray. Amen.

Declaration

I will listen to the right voice.

-2-

What Christ Did

"Do not think that I came to abolish the Law or the Prophets; I did not come to abolish but to fulfill."
Matthew 5:17 NASB

Now that we have established how important it is to believe the correct voice. Let's start by laying one essential foundational stone, for, without it, we cannot build anything that would last. Believing the proper voice is probably the most critical thing to a believer. Our Heavenly Father wants us to believe Him. We can't believe Him if we don't believe what He said about Jesus, "This is the work of God, that you believe in Him whom He has sent." John 6:29 (NASB) Without knowing what Christ did and what it means for those that are in Christ, the following designations would be pointless.

I used to have this thinking that if only I could be "good" enough, then I will be able to receive good and blessings from God. This thought pattern probably came from my own life and how I grew up. If you do good, you get rewarded, that's what I saw in my life. Then I would find myself reading passages like the one found in Isaiah 64:6. The New Living Translation puts it this way "We are all infected and impure with sin. When we display our righteous deeds, they are nothing but filthy rags. Like autumn leaves, we wither and fall, and our sins sweep us away like the wind." Reading these types of passages, I remember finding myself often confused. If the scriptures say that we are all impure with sin and that our righteous deeds are filthy rags, where does that leave us? What hope do we have if the filthy rags that are described are a rag that would be used for cleaning oneself or like the rags soiled because of a woman's menstrual cycle? I wasn't trying to be overly gross by the way, but if you look up for yourself the words used in the original language, you will see that is the picture that the scriptures paint. I found myself often feeling hopeless due to my lack of understanding. I mean sure at this point in my faith walk, I knew that Jesus died for my sins, but what did that really mean? It was at first some obscure concept, and due to weak teaching, my identity in Christ suffered.

So ... What did Christ do? I'm glad you asked. Christ did many things for us, so much so that one could write thousands of pages about what He did and still not fully explain all that He did. If I had to sum it up in my own words, I guess I could sum it up in this way. He did what we could not do so that we would not have to rely on our doing. To understand how important this is, we would have to look back again to the fall. As you recall from the previous chapter, the fall of humanity occurred due to failing to listen to the right voice.

A curse is the best description that I could think of that encompasses all the things that happened to humankind due to the fall. A curse that causes, separation from God, death, sickness, pain, suffering, war, violence, death, depravity, poverty, need, destitution, foolishness, weakness, shame, contempt, dishonor, reproach, blame hardship condemnation, humiliation, bad luck, adversity, and more. The list goes on and on never stopping. Every bad thing that happens in this existence occurred as a result of the fall.

I'm sure at this point, you are saying to yourself, "Yea, that's not helping me understand what Christ did." Don't worry; I'm getting there. As I said, Christ did what we could not do. He did it! So, what did He do? He broke the curse by fulfilling the requirements of God, the Father's law.

You see, God is perfect, and His creation was also perfect before the fall of man. When humanity decided to listen to the wrong voice and act on what they heard, they lost their place of righteousness. God, as revealed in the Bible, is Holy, Holy, Holy. He is trice, Holy. He is a God that is righteous, and His kingdom stands due to His righteousness. "Righteousness and justice are the foundation of Your throne; Lovingkindness and truth go before You." Psalm 89:14 NASB. Without righteousness, the entire creation will collapse. Romans 7:12 states it this way "So then, the Law is holy, and the commandment is holy and righteous and good" NASB. His law is holy and blameless. His law is perfect. What is His law? His Word is His law. He is a God whose very presence demands righteousness, and because of that one cannot be where God is without righteousness.

Here comes Jesus on the scene, God in the Flesh. Jesus was the only human to ever live that entirely in all ways fulfilled all of God's law. "Do not think that I came to abolish the Law or the Prophets; I did not come to abolish but to fulfill. – Matthew 5:17 NASB. To say that He fully satisfied the law of God says two different things. First, it says He was perfect according to everything the law requires. Second, He fully satisfied the judgment and wrath of God, becoming the unblemished sacrifice. In the very last book of the Bible, we find the book of Revelations. It is in this book that we find the coronation of the King of existence through His sacrifice. Try to imagine the throne room of God for a moment. A vast, immaculate room with thousands of thousands of angels and creatures all worshiping Him who alone sits on the throne. The most beautiful lavish sight one would ever be able to behold. The pavement you are standing on is pure gold; the colors, smells, and views are all beautiful. My words and images cannot begin to do it justice, so I will just share what the Bible says about this event.

"Then I saw in the right hand of him who sat on the throne a scroll with writing on both sides and sealed with seven seals. And I saw a mighty angel proclaiming in a loud voice, "Who is worthy to break the seals and open the scroll?" But no one in heaven or on earth or under the earth could open the scroll or even look inside it. I wept and wept because no one was found who was worthy to open the scroll or look inside. Then one of the elders said to me, "Do not weep! See, the Lion of the tribe of Judah, the Root of David, has triumphed. He is able to open the scroll and its seven seals." Then I saw a Lamb, looking as if it had been slain, standing at the center of the throne, encircled by the four living creatures and the elders. The Lamb had seven horns and seven eyes, which are the seven spirits[a] of God sent out into all the earth. He went and took the scroll from the right hand of him who sat on the throne. And when he had taken it, the four living creatures and the twenty-four elders fell down before the Lamb. Each one had a harp and they were holding golden bowls full of incense, which are the prayers of God's people. And they sang a new song, saying: "You are worthy to take the scroll and to open its seals, because you were slain, and with your blood you

purchased for God persons from every tribe and language and people and nation. You have made them to be a kingdom and priests to serve our God, and they will reign[b] on the earth." Then I looked and heard the voice of many angels, numbering thousands upon thousands, and ten thousand times ten thousand. They encircled the throne and the living creatures and the elders. In a loud voice they were saying: "Worthy is the Lamb, who was slain, to receive power and wealth and wisdom and strength and honor and glory and praise!" Then I heard every creature in heaven and on earth and under the earth and on the sea, and all that is in them, saying: "To him who sits on the throne and to the Lamb be praise and honor and glory and power, for ever and ever!" The four living creatures said, "Amen," and the elders fell down and worshiped. Revelation 5 NIV

Because He fully satisfied the law of God, we who believe in Him are no longer under the curse. He became a curse so that we would not be cursed. The scripture states, "Christ hath redeemed us from the curse of the law, being made a curse for us: for it is written, Cursed is every one that hangeth on a tree" Galatians 3:13 KJV. No longer are we under the curse. In the following chapters, you will begin to see all the blessings we have in Christ because we are no longer cursed.

Prayer

Father, I thank You that You tell me that I am no longer cursed. I thank You that Jesus became the curse for me so that I could be blessed. I thank You that You now have the conduit through which all Your goodness can flow to me. I thank You also, Father because You are teaching me that it is not about what I do but what Christ did on my behalf. I thank You that surely goodness and mercy shall follow me all of my days. Please continue to open my heart to what You are saying. Help me to listen to Your voice and Your voice only. Amen.

Declaration

I am no longer cursed. I am blessed.

-3-

I Am In Christ

"In that day you will know that I am in My Father,
and you in Me, and I in you."
John 14:20 NASB

Our very first official designation is that we are in Christ; we are hidden. I know that may seem like two designations but hang in with me a bit longer it will make perfect sense soon. Grasping the concept that we are in Christ will make everything else that follows come to life in a way that will radically transform your life and your world. Jesus Himself said that we are in Him. John 14:20. Allow me to paint a picture for you about how I look at what it means to God in saying that we are in Christ. Imagine with me for a second someone having to go through heart surgery to receive a transplant. The patient is on the surgery table, their chest cavity is open, the doctors are wearing their surgical garbs, and the surgery commences. For hours, the doctors are working hard with the help of several other hands to make sure this is a success. The medical instruments are beeping and measuring the patient's vitals, you hear nothing else but breathing and the directions given by the surgeon. Valve by valve, the new heart is placed within the host. When the surgery is completed and the patient is all stitched up, you no longer see the other person's heart because it has now become hidden by the freshly stapled flesh which surrounds it. The doctors let out a sigh of relief and are smiling for a job well done. All that is now seen is the person in which the heart was placed in.

That is kind of how it is for us. We who are in Christ are no longer seen by God as we currently are in this body of sin. The very thing that makes us who we are is still there but, we with, all our faults and sins are not seen because currently in our timeline, the Father only sees Jesus and His Blood. God is outside of the confines of time, so while we may look at things linear, He can see time in its entirety all at the same moment. Not only does He witness who we are at what we consider to be "now," but He also sees our new glorified bodies in eternity. When He looks at the "current" us in Christ, His eyes go to the cross. For it is the cross of Christ that has allowed us to be placed in Christ. The idea of being hidden in Christ is likened to a child hiding under a blanket thinking the things outside the blanket cant see them, or better yet Jesus himself painted the picture of a hen gathering her chicks under her wings - Luke 13:34. In Psalm 91, the Psalmist says, "Whoever dwells in the shelter of the Most High will rest in the shadow of the Almighty." There are also further instances of this idea of being hidden. In the Old Testament, there was an account of the children of Israel when they were slaves in Egypt. One-night God told

Moses that He was going to pass through and strike down the Egyptians. He also told Moses that He would see the blood on the top and the two side posts and pass over the door. God said, "He will not allow the destroyer to enter your houses and strike you down," Exodus 12:23 Berean Study Bible. In order for this to happen, God gave Moses some instructions on what to do. He told him to kill a lamb and put its blood on the doorpost and because of the blood, those who are hidden behind it will not be touched. Imagine a night filled with countless screams and howling of parents losing their children. I don't know if the children of Israel had confidence in the safety that the blood provided, but when all was said and done, they were still alive.

What does the first Passover have to do with being in Christ or Hidden? It has everything to do with it. You see, those who are in Christ are there because of His blood. They were protected that first Passover because of the blood which was speaking out on their behalf. You see, long before CSI existed and DNA was discovered, God knew that blood has a voice. Today countless murders and crimes are solved because of the voice that one's blood carries. Want further proof? In Genesis, we behold the first murder ever to happen when Cain murdered Able. In the account which can be located in Genesis 4:9-10 God asked Cain "where is your brother?" It was not that He didn't know where he was but because He already knew what Cain did, I believe that God wanted to teach us something important. God told Cain "I hear your brother's blood calling out". Now the Bible doesn't describe what the blood was saying but I could imagine that it was saying something along the lines of "Murderer! Avenge Me! Guilty! Blood for Blood!" and all other sorts of condemning accusations. The same way that Abel's Blood had a voice that was demanding payment for what his brother did, the Blood of Jesus speaks out for those who are in Christ. The book of Hebrews puts it this way so that we could clearly understand "and to Jesus, the mediator of a new covenant, and to the sprinkled blood, which speaks better than the blood of Abel." Hebrews 12:24 NASB So what does the Blood of Jesus say for those who are hidden? I'm glad you are still reading, and you want to know. The Blood of Jesus is proclaiming all that we are in Him.

Every designation that you read in this book and all of those that I did not even cover, that is what the Blood is saying. The Blood of Christ has its own voice and it is crying out louder than any other accusation in the seen or unseen world. "Covered by My Blood! Vindicated! Redeemed! Sanctified! Holy! Pure! Righteous! Loved! Protected! Honored! Rich! Strong! Wise!" I could go on and on about what the Blood is saying about us. So, as we continue on this journey, let us always be reminded that because we are in Christ, His Blood is also speaking on our behalf.

The benefits of being in Christ are many but let us take a few moments to focus on a few. We already touched on what the Blood does, but what does that mean to you and me? Well, knowing that God sees Jesus when He looks at us ought to give us the courage and confidence to run to Him and not from Him. I remember reading in Genesis about Adam hiding from God, he hid because he was ashamed. The Blood makes it so that we who are in Christ must no longer be ashamed because all our sins were paid for, and since payment has been made, there is now no condemnation. Don't believe me? Read it for yourself in Romans, chapter 8. Do you need further proof? Here are 3 places that you can find in the scriptures that God tells us that all of our sins are paid for. (Hebrews 10:17; Jeremiah 31:34 & Isaiah 43:25) Let me be crystal clear if I wasn't already clear enough when

God says "ALL" He means "ALL." That means all of your past, present, and future sins were, are, and will forever be forgiven. Remember, God is outside the confines of time. I know that there are circles out there that believe this kind of thinking is going to lead people to think that it is OK to sin. Trust me when I tell you the more you realize who you are in Christ, the more you will live a godly life, and by no effort of your own may I add. Remember it's all about Christ and what He did for us so that no man can boast.

Paul, one of the writers of the New Testament wrote to a church one time and worded it like this, "For by grace you have been saved through faith; and that not of yourselves, it is the gift of God; not as a result of works, so that no one may boast. For we are His workmanship, created in Christ Jesus for good works, which God prepared beforehand so that we would walk in them." Ephesians 2:8-10 NASB. You can also find it said, "But by His doing you are in Christ Jesus, who became to us wisdom from God, and righteousness and sanctification, and redemption, 1 Corinthians 1:30 NASB. So, run to God because "The LORD is near to all who call upon Him, To all who call upon Him in truth." Psalm 145:18 NASB The truth is His Word, which states, "In him and through faith in him, we may approach God with freedom and confidence." Ephesians 3:12 NIV.

I pray that because you now know you are in Christ, hidden, and the Blood of Christ testifies on your behalf, that it enables you to run often to the loving arms of our Father.

Prayer

Father, I thank You that You have revealed to me that I am in Christ, that I am hidden, and because of that, You have shown me that when You look at me, all you see is Your perfect Son and

His precious Blood. I thank You that the Blood of Jesus, cries out for me, it has declared what You want it to say over my life. I thank You that You don't only see me for what I currently am, but You see me as I am in Your Son and what I will be like in eternity. I thank You that my very presence no longer offends You, and it's all because of Your love for us that You gave us Your Son so that we could be close to you again. Amen.

Declaration

God said I am in Christ; I am Hidden; I believe it. God said it. Who am I to argue with God?

-4-

I Am Saved

"For by grace you have been saved through faith; and that not of yourselves, it is the gift of God; not as a result of works, so that no one may boast."
Ephesians 2:8-9 NASB

What does it mean to be saved? Rescued? Recovered? Liberated? Oh, I know, maybe, born again? The thought of being saved can cause you to think and conjure up many mental images. Picture the following for a moment with me. It is the middle of July, you are enjoying the sun while you lie on the beach. The sun is hot, the skies are blue, and you are just getting that well-deserved rest after a long hard, stressful week at work. Kids are running around you playing in the sand, you have some cold refreshing drinks near you, and you are jamming out to that summer play-list that you worked on for hours last night. Your eyelids are heavy, and your head begins to nod, but just then, you are abruptly woken up by yelling, "Help! Help! Someone help us!" Startled, you jump right up to see what is going on. People are frantically running to the shore, the screaming continues, and there is commotion everywhere. Finally, you witness what is going on. Far off into the distance, you see a young child struggling because of the strong waves. The mother is crying hysterically but, help is on the way. The lifeguard is swimming towards the child, and it looks like everything is going to be OK. As you watch what is unfolding, heart pounding from the tension, the atmosphere goes from assurance of rescue to confusion. As you watch the lifeguard stops swimming towards the child whose arms are desperately waving in a panic. You notice the mother, she appears to be in shock because she doesn't know what is going on, you imagine she is asking why isn't this lifeguard saving her child? Is there something wrong with the lifeguard? Are they injured? Are they stuck? The lifeguard is too far out into the water to honestly know what is going on. The child begins to lose momentum in their arms, and the atmosphere is even tenser. Finally, the child's arms stop moving, and all hope seems to vanish. The mother losing her composure collapses to the ground, sitting on the hot sand looking totally defeated. Motionless thinking about the fact that her child is gone. Just then, when all hope seemed to be lost, the lifeguard once again begins to swim toward the child and the watching crowd clamors and begins to cheer. The lifeguard makes it to the child, rescue complete. But, wait, is it too late? The crowd is stunned, and a great silence has fallen over them. Standing in suspense, they wait for the lifeguard and the child to be on dry ground. They make it back to the shore, and the mother is there as still dealing with the shock of unbelief; after all, she believed her baby was gone. But her baby was not gone. Her child was alive and well because the lifeguard saved them. "Mommy! Mommy!" the child cried out for their mother. Being hugged tightly in their mother's arms, the child began to tell her, "This man told me to calm down and don't panic, he told me to stop moving my arms because he was going to save me and that I could count on him. I was scared, but I believed him, and because of that, I am safe."

When I was a teen, I used to be a lifeguard. One of the things that I remember learning during training was that the person you are saving is often the one who makes the decision if they are actually going to be saved or not. When a person is drowning and panicking, it makes it very hard for the rescue party to save them without putting themselves in danger. If possible, the lifeguard would attempt to speak with the person they are trying to rescue in order to calm them down. If that is not possible, they would have to wait until the person is exhausted from trying things on their own, then swoop in for the save. This is probably something that everyone has seen in their life, be in a movie or at a beach or pool. Frankly, I could have used anything. Be it this example, a Firefighter saving someone from a burning building or even some strong superhero saving someone from a building that is about to crumble on their heads. All of those examples are vivid examples of a person being saved, and now that you have a picture of what it is to be saved, let us look at what it means when Christians say they are saved.

Here is bible 101 for you. The New Testament was written initially in mostly Greek. In the Greek, the Word that is used for saved is "Sozo," and it literally means "to save, rescue, heal." In the Bible, the Word saved is often used with God as the subject. For example, "the God who saves" He is the God that rescues His people. If He states that we are saved by Him, who are we to dispute it. To see ourselves as saved, we first need to know that Christ is the savior of the world - John 4:42. To better understand this, I'm going to answer a few questions. What are we saved from? Why does He save? Who does He save, and can I lose my salvation?

What are we saved from? If you remember back to the chapter about what Christ did, we covered a few of those things. So, we won't be going into it as deeply, ultimately, what didn't He save us from? But for the purpose of this chapter, I will be focusing on the fact that He saved us from sin and being separated God the Father. Still, you can rely on Him to save you from whatever it is you need saving from. I think about the disciples crying out, "LORD, SAVE US!" While the winds and the waves were beating the boat, and Jesus was just sleeping. You can find that in Matthew 8:25. I think of the kings whose words have been recorded in the scripture calling out to be saved and rescued. "I called out to the Lord, and he saved me" Psalm 34:6 You were also saved from the old ways of thinking, saved from death, saved from the law, saved from curses, saved from how you see yourself and more. There are many examples of what we could be saved from, but the most important thing is to know that if there is something that you need to be saved from, Jesus is the savior for it.

Why does He save? Let me be honest in saying I don't fully understand all the things of the Lord, but I can tell you what His Word has to say about why He saves. I think one of the best ways to understand why He saves is to look at the Children of Israel when they were still in Egyptian captivity. The parallels that they have with the Church will hopefully shed some light on this mystery. There they were a nation of people enslaved to the Egyptians, crying out, longing to be saved from their captivity. It was during this time that the

Scriptures state, "And now the cry of the Israelites has reached me, and I have seen the way the Egyptians are oppressing them" Exodus 3:9 NIV. I bet you are wondering what that verse has to do with why He saves, hang in with me a little bit longer. You see, according to history, the Egyptians were the power of the world. During this time, there was no other power that would dare challenge them, or so they thought. Our Heavenly Father was setting up to show them that He was indeed the Most High God. In Psalm 106, the marvelous deliverance from Egypt is recounted, and in verse 8, we find why. I told you I'd get to it. "...Nevertheless, He saved them for His name's sake, that He might make His power known." The word power denotes strength and might. We are saved so that our God can show Himself strong to the world. There is a verse that is quoted by one of the New Testament writers, and it says, "To whom has the arm of the Lord been revealed?" John 12:38. Every time I read that verse or the verse that it quotes in the Old Testament, I think of a very strong person flexing their muscles. A purist may say that I am twisting the scriptures and say that the "Arm of the Lord" that is being referred to here is none other than a reference to Jesus. I would agree with them, but I will also challenge them by asking, isn't the strength of God, Jesus? Another way to put it is by saying God "Flexed" on them. For out of all of the miracles that one could imagine, I would say that the greatest is for a person to be saved. Man can't save himself if he could, then Christ would have never had to come. But cheer up "What is impossible with man is possible with God" Luke 18:27. It is His strength that is showing Him to be entirely just, righteous and loving at the same time.

Who does He save? Everyone who allows themselves to be saved. What? My story at the beginning of this chapter didn't paint a good enough picture? OK, then let us look at the scriptures beginning with what is probably the most well-known verse in all of scripture. "For God so loved the world that He gave His one and only Son, that whoever believes in Him shall not perish but have eternal life" John 3:16 NIV. Again, in John 1:12 It states, "But to all who believed Him and accepted Him, He gave the right to become children of God. Romans 10:9-10 puts it this way "If you declare with your mouth, "Jesus is Lord," and believe in your heart that God raised Him from the dead, you will be saved. For it is with your heart that you believe and are justified, and it is with your mouth that you profess your faith and are saved."

Lastly, can I lose my salvation? I touched a bit on my personal salvation story, and I have to say that it has been many years since I was gripped by His love, and I am still learning about His love for me. I don't always walk in the victory won for me at the cross, but I can say that the most significant thing that I learned about salvation is that it is forever! Not from the moment you accept Jesus until the moment you mess up, but let me repeat, FOREVER! I have been around people and places who would teach that you can lose your salvation because of a verse in Revelation about losing the crown of life. As I have stated several times throughout this book, I don't claim to know everything but allow me to ask you this, were you able to undo what Adam did by your good works? Come on, think about it. OK, let me answer that for you, NO. So, what makes you think that you are strong enough or have the ability to undo what Christ did? Christ looked at EVERY sin you ever committed between the dashes on your headstone and still basically said: "I got this. I'm going to die for all of those sins." Jesus doesn't tell us the moment we accept Him "OK, I took the sins of your past; you got it from here." When Christ yelled "It Is Finished" (John 19:30) on the cross, that's precisely what it was, finished! His saving

37

work was complete for those who would believe in the gift of God.

Prayer

I thank You, Father, that You have saved me by your mighty hand. I thank You that no matter how much I struggled to rescue myself, You had the wisdom to wait until I didn't have any more strength in myself for You to swoop in and rescue me. You have saved me, You rescued me, and You healed me. You are the perfect savior. I thank You that You have revealed Your strength to me. Amen.

Declaration

I am Saved by the blood of the lamb, not by what I do but by what Christ did. I believe it, and nothing can take it away from me.

-5-

I Am Redeemed

*"Let the redeemed of the LORD say so, Whom He has
redeemed from the hand of the adversary"*
Psalm 107:2 NASB

The cell is dank and dreary. The floor is impenetrable, merely stepping on it sends a chill up your spine. The place to lie down can hardly be called a bed. The walls are lifeless and dull. There are no windows that allow in any natural light, and the steel bars are the epitome of the lifelessness, this is the situation faced by those who are sentenced to prison, which any one would consider to be hell on earth.

Before accepting the gift of our Father everyone is in this prison, and you are a prisoner to the one whom Adam forfeited the title deed. In the garden when Adam and Eve chose to listen to the serpent, they had to deal with the consequences of their choice, and the main underlining consequence was that now the entire human race and all of God's creation legally belonged to another master. This master was not gracious and only cared about trying to hurt and dethrone God. This master was a steward of God's righteousness and knew that if he could get God to break His Word, then God can no longer be God. So, the serpent in his craftiness thought he had God painted into a corner. I'm sure he knew how much God loved humanity and truly believed God would break His own law for them. That was not the case; God had bigger plans, something that a being with limited knowledge would have no way of knowing what was coming. The enemy knew the penalty that humankind had to pay was either blood or death, and he now had the right to demand payment. All seemed lost, but the Father had Jesus, our Kinsman Redeemer.

What is a redeemer, and why does it matter to who you are in Christ? To truly understand that, let us talk about what redemption is. The Word redeemed comes from the idea of being brought back, being purchased. Think about a kidnapper holding someone for ransom; that is how it was for anyone without the gift of God that is Christ. God's law is absolute, and His Word will come to pass. When Adam and Eve chose to listen to the wrong voice, they had to pay the penalty, which was death. God told them if they eat from the fruit of the tree of knowledge of good and evil, they will surely die. In order to defer the time in which the payment would be due, God killed an animal and used its skin to cover Adam and Eve. That initial covering was a foreshadow of the covering we would have in Christ. This initial payment bought them some time. Ever since then, that same sentence has been upon the human race. Several chapters ago, I spoke about this with regards to Abel and how his blood cried out, and God heard it. This is so important I will repeat it here; the blood of Jesus cries out on our behalf, saying, "Redeemed!" Blood was the only thing that could satisfy the payment. You see, God is holy and just and righteous, and there was only one way He could fully satisfy His judgment, and just wrath. He had to provide Himself a lamb.

To know why that matters, one would have to look through the pages of Leviticus to find the account of the law of redemption. We can find details about the law of redemption in Leviticus 25, and within that chapter, you will discover that it covers both loss of property and the loss of freedom. Adam and, in turn, all of humankind lost both property and freedom when listening to the wrong voice in the garden. From that moment, we were prisoners, and only our Kinsman Redeemer could save us. According to Leviticus, a Kinsman Redeemer had to have several qualifications to meet the requirements. They had to be qualified, willing, and able.

To be considered qualified, they had to be a next of kin or relative. Jesus is our brother as you can see in Hebrews 2:11 NLT "So now, Jesus and the ones he makes holy have the same Father. That is why Jesus is not ashamed to call them his brothers and sisters." Again, in Hebrews 2:17 the scriptures say "Therefore, it was necessary for him to be made in every respect like us, his brothers and sisters, so that he could be our merciful and faithful High Priest before God. Then he could offer a sacrifice that would take away the sins of the people."

Next, was the question about being able. Did He have the means, power and authority to pay the price? He is able as you can see in the previous text. His ableness reminds me of an account in Gospels that can find in (Mark 9:17-27) in this account we find a father who had a demonized son and long story short the father was at his wits end, he did everything he knew he could do and nothing seemed to work. Finally, he took his son to Jesus and told Jesus, "if you are able, heal him" Jesus did just that He healed him. So, in the healing of the young boy, again, Jesus shows His ableness.

The final prerequisite was that the person had to be willing. There are many examples of where we find Jesus showing that he is willing. Jesus is the willing servant of the Father to do that which the Father has willed for him. In Isaiah 42:1-4, there is a prophecy about the servant of God who "in faithfulness will bring forth justice." In the Gospel of Mark, Jesus is quoted as stating, "For even the Son of Man did not come to be served, but to serve, and to give his life as a ransom for many." – Mark 10:45 (NIV), and again in (Luke 5:12-13) we see that Jesus is willing when a man who was covered in leprosy said to him "Lord if you are willing to make me clean," to which Jesus responded: "I am willing, be clean."

If you want to continue to study about a kinsman redeemer, I would suggest you take a look at the Book of Ruth in it you will meet a redeemer named Boaz, as great a redeemer Boaz was Jesus is the greatest redeemer. He has redeemed us, and it was completed at the moment He cried out on the cross "Finished!" in which you could read all about in John 19:28-30.

Now that you know what it means to be redeemed and how you are redeemed, let look at how that changes your life. In Revelations 5:12, we are invited to peek into some of the events of heaven, and here we witness a lamb, and it is said that this lamb is worthy, "worthy is the lamb that was slaughtered to receive... Those things that Jesus received are the things that He purchased for us with His blood. In our redemption, everything Christ has, we have in Him. Every facet of our old life is redeemed. Joel 2:23-27 shows us that our entire situation is redeemed. Our Redeemer lives (Job 5:25) and we are redeemed from:

- Impotence to power, from not having authority or effectiveness in what I say, to a place of power because of what God says and what God says happens (Isaiah 55:11)

- From poverty, need, lack, or destitution to riches. From never having to having enough to being able to be a blessing to have enough for every good work. (Zechariah) 8:13

- From foolishness to wisdom. Jesus has become our wisdom (1 Corinthians 1:30)

- From weakness, lack of physical strength, sickness feebleness to might. Jesus never went to someone and said "you are too healthy here is some sickness" NEVER did that happen (Isaiah 53:5 & Psalms 28:7) what He said was "the well don't need a doctor, only the sick" Mark (2:17)

- From contempt, dishonor, reproach, blemish, condemnation and, humiliation to honor. There is now no condemnation for those who are in Christ Jesus (Romans 8:1)

- From shame, blame (being blamed for bad) & dishonor to Glory (being credited for Good). We carry the Glory of God people will say they are blessed because you are around Genesis 12:2

- From curses, hardship, bad luck, adversity, calamity, doom & gloom to blessing. All of Gods promises are yes and amen in Christ Jesus (2 Corinthians 1:20

You and I are a peculiar people in the sense that nothing else in all of creation can stake the claim that they are the redeemed of the Lord except us. Those are just a few things we are redeemed from. The more you read the Word, the more you will find for yourself. Being redeemed is not something that we earned, so it's also not something we can lose. Man's "good works didn't do it, we were hostages, and our hero paid the ransom and more so that we can be redeemed because of His sacrificial love and grace. To say that Jesus paid the price would be an understatement, honestly, He overpaid and was happy to do it because it was His purpose to redeem us. We are those called according to his purpose (Romans 8:28-30.)

Prayer

Father, I thank You that You did not hold back Your Son from being slaughtered on our behalf to become the agent of our redemption. I thank You that His blood is what was used as payment and because we are redeemed, You will not hold any good thing from us. I thank you that

You have done, are doing, and will do everything You have pledged to do to and for us in Christ. I thank You that I am the redeemed of the Lord. I thank You that You have made me wealthy, wise, strong, honored, glorified, and blessed. I thank You, Father, for Jesus. Amen.

Declaration

I Am the redeemed of the Lord.

-6-

I Am Qualified

"Giving thanks to the Father, who has qualified you to share in the inheritance of the saints in the kingdom of light."
Colossians 1:12 NIV.

Have you ever been told that you are not enough? It doesn't feel good, does it? Growing up, I experienced that more than I would like to admit. I remember being at a party, and a good friend of mine asked me a question, he asked me, "Does it bother you when your own people act as though you are not enough?" You see, he was just in Puerto Rico, and being from N.Y., they consider you to be a "New Yorican." I began thinking about this, and for the next two days, I couldn't shake the thought. Being a person of mixed descent, I had the blessing of my family coming from two different nations.

My dad's family is Dominican, and my mother's family is Puerto Rican. I can remember times that I was treated as if I was not Puerto Rican enough for other Puerto Ricans. Nor was I Dominican enough for my fellow Dominicans. Thinking back, I was often treated as if I was never American enough (though I was born and raised in the U.S.) to my fellow Americans. I've even experienced what could be seen as trivial moments of not being athletic enough to be selected first in pickup games in any sport. Being born in Buffalo and raised for most of my childhood in the Bronx, I was never Buffalo enough or never N.Y. enough. I even used to think I was not enough for my dad since he was not in my life. Times I didn't get the job or didn't even get called in for an interview. Times when I didn't get into my first choice of school, or when I got turned down by a lady I was pursuing, I didn't think I was enough, even not being Christian enough for other Christians. I'm sure that I could go on forever if I really tried, but then we would never make it to our next designation. As I pondered the idea of not being enough, I settled on the fact that for someone to tell you that you are not enough was them really telling you that they don't accept you. Well, I have good news for you, and I would like to share it with you. In Christ, you are accepted, and it is God Himself that qualifies you. Our Father says we "are a chosen race, a royal priesthood, a holy nation, a people for God's own possession, so that you may proclaim the excellencies of Him who has called you out of darkness into His marvelous light; for you once were not a people, but now you are the people of God; you had not received mercy, but now you have received mercy" 1 Peter 2:9-10 NASB

"But, But But, you don't know me. You don't know what I have done." I'm confident that many people are reading this who have this exact thought. Good news! It doesn't matter! Jesus paid the price to qualify you. Right now, because of Jesus' blood, you qualify for all of God's blessings. So, don't believe the lie that you are not good enough. The blood of Jesus is what makes you good enough. Nothing else ever can!

Throughout the pages of this book, I have been talking about the importance of hearing the correct voice. When you think or feel that you are not enough or that you are not accepted, listen to what the Father has to say about you. In Colossians 1:12, the NIV states it this way, "giving thanks to the Father, who has qualified you ..." Think about that for a moment, He qualifies us! And if God qualifies us, we will always and forever be enough, we will be accepted for all eternity. How could the God of the universe qualify us? He does it by making us righteous.

Being righteous, or in right standing with God is all the qualification you need, and righteousness is a free gift that you receive when you receive Jesus Christ. I stated this before but it is worth repeating, it is not due to what you have done but instead based on what Jesus did for you. Let me put it this way, you don't become qualified with God based on your performance, you were MADE qualified by God when you received Jesus. Romans 5:17 says, "Righteousness is not something you have earned or done, but a gift given by God." In fact, Jesus is your righteousness. In 1 Corinthians verse 30, the NIV puts it this way, "It is because of him that you are in Christ Jesus, who has become for us wisdom from God -- that is, our righteousness, holiness, and redemption." Need more proof? In 2 Corinthians 5:21, it states, "God made him who had no sin to be sin for us so that in him we might become the righteousness of God." You don't have to do anything else so you can qualify. It's a gift! You just have to believe it!

I know, I know, this is supposed to be a chapter about you being enough or qualified how did this turn into learning about being righteous? There was just no way for me to talk about one without the other. Think of it this way you got a bonus designation that you didn't pay for (pun intended)

Let's get back to talking about us being qualified. What exactly are we qualified for? Well, to start, we are qualified as our main verse says, "to share in the inheritance of the saints in the kingdom of light." This inheritance is all that God has. This inheritance makes all of His promises ours. Take a look at 2 Corinthians 1:20 with me. "For no matter how many promises God has made, they are "Yes" in Christ. And so through him the "Amen" is spoken by us to the glory of God." It also includes but is not limited to being qualified and accepted as His Children. Being qualified to receive any and every blessing from God. Being qualified for His goodness and graciousness towards us. Being qualified to be completely forgiven. Qualified to be filled with God's Holy Spirit. Qualified to receive healing. Qualified to get our prayers answered. Qualified to prosper and never have lack. Qualified to live with God on Earth and in Heaven. We are qualified for any and every promise from God.

Prayer

Father, I thank You that You have and continue to qualify me. You have qualified me by making me righteous through Jesus. I thank You that all of Your promises are mine and that You did all this to show me how much You loved me. I thank You that I don't have to go through this world with feelings of never being enough or accepted as You accept me in Jesus. I thank You that You have chosen me. You call me a royal priesthood, a holy nation, and a person for Your own possession. I thank You that I am qualified to receive Your mercy and love. I thank You for Your Word, and I choose to believe what You say. Amen.

Declaration

I am qualified for all God's blessings. God made me qualified!

I Am Justified

"Or do you not know that wrongdoers will not inherit the kingdom of God? Do not be deceived: Neither the sexually immoral nor idolaters nor adulterers nor men who have sex with men[a] 10 nor thieves nor the greedy nor drunkards nor slanderers nor swindlers will inherit the kingdom of God. 11 And that is what some of you were. But you were washed, you were sanctified, you were justified in the name of the Lord Jesus Christ and by the Spirit of our God."
1 Corinthians 6:9-11 NASB

I know that I have typically used a single verse to open up until now, but it was vital for me to use these verses for this chapter. Let me start by saying this is one of my favorite portions of scripture. I love it so much because I was most of the things on that list, I read these words, and they changed my life. In this portion of scripture, you find a list of things done; then, you find the word "but" that small three-letter world revolutionized my faith. You see, in the English language, that short term negates everything that came before it. In other words, no matter what you were, no matter how bad you were and what you did, none of it mattered anymore if the blood of Jesus washed you. If you have been born again, you are a new creation. You have been justified and made just as if you or I have never sinned. Justification is a legal term that means the act of declaring something righteous in the eyes of God. When God looks at us since we are in Christ, He sees us just as Christ is, NOT GUILTY! Christ fulfilled the law, and the judgment that was due to me was placed on Christ at the cross. Yes, "For all have sinned and fall short of the glory of God" Romans 3:23 but Our Father is not a God who sits on His throne looking to zap people with lightning bolts or make bad things happen to us when we sin (which by the way literally means "missing the mark"). We all miss the mark, and that is why we need Jesus.

Jesus is the one who hit the mark and shows us to God as justified. Romans 5:9 puts it this way "Since we have now been justified by his blood, how much more shall we be saved from God's wrath through him!" New International Version.

If you take a look at the entire fourth chapter of Romans, you will find that Abraham was a man who was also justified. It shows us that he was justified by faith. We must look at why the Bible teaches us that Abraham was justified by faith, because then and only then can we understand that being called justified by God is truly a gift. Abraham, who many consider being the Father of their faith around the world, was once told by God to take his Son and sacrifice him. You see, in those times, child sacrifice was not abnormal; it was very commonplace actually. It is possible that Abram, (which was his name before being called out by God) was accustomed to seeing children sacrificed. After all, it is said that

Abraham's father, Terah, was a high priest (his name means priest) in a land that worshiped many gods. (Joshua 24:2)

Now I'm not saying that the following is true, but I would like to submit a theory to you, or rather ask you a question. If Terah was a high priest of other gods, is it possible that Abraham witnessed his father sacrifice one of his own sons? The following is all conjecture, but I think it is a reasonable theory because after all, Abraham left his father's house and took his nephew Lot with him. Now I wasn't there, and again it is just a theory on my behalf, but based on what the scriptures show, the facts are Lot left with his uncle. Where was Lot's father and why was Abram so willing to take him?

With all that said, there is this account of God showing Abram that his descendants will be like the numbers of the stars and the grains of sand, but there was one problem Abram was old, and he didn't have any children. Come on, God said that to a man who had zero children naturally? Look at what happened next; his wife tells him, "look, I am old, and I can't have children"... There goes that listening to the wrong voice again. She tells him, "sleep with my maidservant so that you could have an heir." Abram went willingly ... like a sheep being led to slaughter. So, he slept with the maidservant, and she got pregnant. (You could read the rest of the drama unfold in Genesis 16)

To no one's surprise, that fixed NOTHING for Abraham because now his wife, who was the one who came up with the idea, though Abraham did not fight it at all, was mad. She wasn't like "sleep on the couch" mad; she was furious to the point that she wanted to kick her pregnant servant out of the country. That was not all; she also wanted the son whom Abraham had longed for, gone as well. God intervened and did not let that happen.

Sara, though she was once barren, was promised by God that she too would bear a child. Genesis 21 tells the story about how the Lord was gracious to Sarah, just as He said he would be, He did for Sarah what He had promised to do, and she was redeemed from her barrenness. After some time, Sarah was in her feelings and again kicked her maidservant out, but this time God allowed it to happen, and that brings us back to why God called Abraham justified.

Abraham was now down to one son, and God comes and says, "Take now your son, your only son Isaac, whom you love, and go to the land of Moriah, and offer him there as a burnt offering on one of the mountains of which I shall tell you." Genesis 22:2 King James Version. As the account goes on, Abraham sets out with his son, some fire, a knife, his servants, and donkey. On the way, he tells his servants to go home and that they will return in a few days. As they went on, Abraham's son noticed that something was missing; the lamb that was supposed to be slaughtered for the sacrifice. (He was aware of the practice already.) The son said to his dad. "dad, I have the wood, you have the fire and the knife, but I don't see the lamb" what's up with that basically? What the son didn't know was what God had told his father to do. Think about this, here is a man who, as I said before, probably witnessed his own father sacrifice his brother, and if not, he was most definitely aware of the custom. Abraham, the man who was called out by God from amongst his people, who were knowns for these practices and was about to do the same thing, yet Abraham believed God. Abraham is quoted as saying, "God himself will provide the lamb for the burnt offering, my son." Genesis 22:8 New International Version.

As they went up the mountain, I could imagine this father believing against all things that even if he kills his son, God has the power to bring him back. They finally get to the peak of the mountain, and the moment of truth has arrived. I imagine Abraham tying up his son and placing him on the altar with tears in his eyes. He probably gagged him because I could imagine he would not want to hear voice of the son he loves voice crying out, asking him, "Why? Please! Don't! What did I do wrong? I thought you said that the Lord Himself would provide a lamb!?" Abraham continued as he lifted up the knife to plunge it into his beautiful baby boy, who was more like a teen if we were being accurate, but you get the picture. As his hands tightly gripped the knife, looking with watery eyes at the place where he is going to stab his precious gift from God, he probably thought to himself, "if it were not for the Lord, I wouldn't even have you." The moment of truth arrived, there was no going back now, as the knife plunges toward the boy, God called out to him, "Abraham!" Almost as if it were a reminder that he was no longer Abram, but that he was seeing the promise that God made to him, and that he saw his redemption right before his eyes. In Genesis 22, God basically told him, "Abraham do not lay a finger on the boy; do not harm him. Now, I know that you would do anything for God. You have not held back from me, your son, your only son. Abraham looked around and there in a bush; he saw a ram caught by its horns. He went over and took the ram, and he sacrificed it as a burnt offering instead of his son.

What does that account have to do with being justified? A lot. In the same way that Abraham was justified, we are justified by our faith in the Son of God. That is why God calls us justified. Abraham believed the voice of God and God wants us to do the same. I will close this chapter with a portion of scripture that I think says it better than I ever could.

21 "But now apart [k]from the law the righteousness of God has been manifested, being witnessed by the Law and the Prophets, 22 even the righteousness of God through faith in Jesus Christ for all those [l]who believe; for there is no distinction; 23 for all [m]have sinned and fall short of the glory of God, 24 being justified as a gift by His grace through the redemption which is in Christ Jesus; 25 whom God displayed publicly as a [n]propitiation [o]in His blood through faith. This was to demonstrate His righteousness, [p]because in the forbearance of God He passed over the sins previously committed; 26 for the demonstration, I say, of His righteousness at the present time, so that He would be just and the justifier of the one who [q]has faith in Jesus. 27 Where then is boasting? It is excluded. By what kind of law? Of works? No, but by a law of faith. 28 [r]For we maintain that a man is justified by faith apart from works [s]of the law. 29 Or is God the God of Jews only? Is He not the God of Gentiles also? Yes, of Gentiles also, 30 since indeed God who will justify the [t]circumcised [u]by faith and the [v]uncircumcised through faith is one. 31 Do we then nullify [w]the law through faith?

May it never be! On the contrary, we establish the law."
Romans 3:21-31 New American Standard Bible

Prayer

Father, I thank You that You consider us justified. You have made us be just as we have never sinned. We thank You that You have given us countless examples of how important it is to listen to the correct voice. We thank You that You tell us that You see Jesus when You look at us. We thank You that You have hidden us in Him. We thank You for loving us so much that You would not even hold back your Son. We thank You in the precious name of Jesus. Amen.

Declaration

I am justified. I am right in the eyes of God.

-8-

I Am Royalty

"but Christ was faithful as a Son over His house-- whose house we are, if we hold fast our confidence and the boast of our hope firm until the end."
Hebrews 3:6 NASB

Throughout human history, those who have amassed massive power and wealth have been able to build their names and family. One could think about the great kingdoms in Egypt. They became dynasties that lasted for several generations, we can think about the regimes in China and even the Royal family in modern-day England. If that is not enough to get you thinking, there are also top-rated shows that portray how families or houses are represented. These great families use crests or banners that denote their great homes. Our main verse for this chapter says we are of His house, so for us who are of House Christ, The Lord Himself is our Banner.

In times past ancient armies would carry banners that indicated whose army it was. It was something that often went before the troops to announce to the enemy what is coming their way. In some cases, it was a huge flag, and in other cases, it was a piece of wood or some sort of hard material, but in all cases, the symbol of the house to whom it belonged was on it.

Let's imagine for a moment that there was a banner-man riding with the banner approaching a foreign army. The foreign military would see the crest or symbol of the house to which it belonged and know that though they only see one person, that specific person has an entire army backing him up. The best part isn't that the army is the strength, it's actually the house for whom the army is fighting for.

I stated earlier that the Lord is our banner. Yahweh Nissi is the name of God that Moses learned about during a battle with the Amalekites. They were a nation that housed lands of fierce warriors, and here were the Hebrews who had just left Egypt. They were not fighters, they were farmers and builders, the working class for the Egyptians. Yet the Lord had a sign that went before them during this time when they left Egypt. There was a pillar of smoke and of fire on their way out, and it went before them showing all the nations before them and behind them to whose house they belonged to. If you care to read more about this account, you can find it in Exodus 17:8-16.

What does any of this have to do with who we are in Christ? A ton. The Lord is our Banner, so He is the one who reflects our ideals, our thoughts, and faith. Imagine again with me for a brief moment, think about all the marketing and banners we see everywhere. The Amazon "Smile," the NIKE Check," The McDonalds M," "Apple's Apple" the list goes on and on. What is the purpose of all that marketing? It is to be a banner so that people could know what they are getting. The Lord is our banner, so the rest of the world will know what they are getting. The scripture says that we are the "light of the world" the "salt of the Earth" (Matthew 5:13-16), and it also says that the world will know that we are Christ's because of our love for one another. (John 13:35)

What exactly makes us part of house Christ? That can be answered in a very short sentence. We are God's children. One of the very 1st things that caused me to fall in love with God was when I learned that He said He will "be a father to the fatherless." (Psalm 68:5) When I was very young in the faith, I came across this message, and it hit home in more ways than one. My biological dad was alive, but he was just never part of my life in any way that I could say actually had value. All I knew I did not want to be like him. Most of us find our identity in what we do or where we come from. Me, for example, some of my identity at that point was an angry fatherless boy lashing out at a single mother who was not many years older than I was. The rest of my identity came from what I didn't have instead of what I did have. I grew up without my dad, and a lot of who I grew up to be, I believe, came from my desire of not wanting to be like a father who would leave his own child.

I always felt like he didn't love me, as if there was something I did that made him go away. I could never figure out what was wrong with me that my dad didn't want to be there. The only childhood memories I had of him were from a time he took me and my cousins to watch Kindergarten Cop at the movie theater. A time when he drove me from New York City to Buffalo and a time I moved to live with him for a few months. I was going into 5th grade, and I moved from New York State out west to California. I was only there a few months, but here I was living with a man that I barely knew. The most significant memory I have from that time was that I tried so hard to make myself more loved by him with everything I did and said.

I didn't live with him long; a few months later, I was headed back to be with my family in New York. Here I was a 10-year-old boy flying across the country all by myself on Thanksgiving. I remember that flight even to this day. I recall the flight attendant feeling so sorry for me, that I was not with my family and didn't have money for anything extra on the flight, that she gave me a turkey Hot Pocket. I have never in my life felt more alone. I have countless stories about my times without my dad, but I'll save those for another time. I share this glimpse into my story because I believe that is where a significant part of my identity crisis came from. I like many in my generation, and demographics may have never known a father's love, but that didn't stop God.

Jesus came to reveal the Father to us, He came to reveal God to us as Father and we as His children. This God, who is the Everlasting Father (Isaiah 9:6) told me, "I will be your Father," (2 Samuel 7:14), He said, He will never leave me nor forsake me (Deuteronomy 31:6). He is our Father, so we are His children, thus making us of His house. So how are we children of God in Christ? You thought I would never get there, right? Well... He adopted us. (Romans 8:14-17) He is the Father who provides, protects, & praises His children. That is the One to whose house we belong. The scriptures teach us that we had a previous caretaker, the world, but no longer because we now have a loving Father. Galatians 3:26 says, "For you are all sons of God through faith in Christ Jesus. Now, this verse does not exclude daughters, so don't worry if you are a lady, and you are reading this book. Our father is inclusive. He loves women the same, if not more? Think about it. He made you ladies after us, version 2.0 and also His Son came in human form, from a lady so He must really think highly of women. Need further proof well I have that too take a look at 2 Corinthians 6:18 with me "And I will be a Father to you, and you shall be sons and daughters to me, says the Lord almighty. Need more proof that you are of house Christ? Philippians 2:15 states, "so that you will prove yourselves to be blameless and guiltless innocent and uncontaminated Children of God without Blemish." We are without blemish because of the pure blood of the lamb. We are in Christ; we are saved, and we are of house Christ. So now that we have established the validity of our claim, and the fact that we are no longer slaves but heirs; think about that, let it sink in. In a culture of microwaving, God is into marinating, so again, let that soak in for a moment. We are heirs to the kingdom of God. What, how could that be? You may have not been born to any mighty house of note or some rich and powerful family yet in Christ we are children of God and being born again "He made us, not we ourselves but He made us Heirs - Psalms 100:3

OK, so we know that we are His children, and that makes us of house Christ, but what are the benefits? All the good we could think of.

There is no lack of benefit as being part of the house. There is an account in scripture that accurately portrays my point. In 2 Samuel 9, you can read about a person who was an orphan that was adopted by the King, and he sat at the table for the rest of his life. Children sit and eat at the table. We aren't orphans who eat in secret with fear of being discovered. We are royalty adopted by the Father, and He wants us to eat at the table that He prepared for us. He wants us to do so without any fear believing that His word is His bond and that because He states we are His children, then we indeed are His children. Another benefit is that we are no longer slaves to the law. We are sons and daughters and are not slaves (Galatians 4:7). When were slaves and not children, the unbearable weight of the law and commands were given to us, but now that we are children of house Christ, grace is present to us. Words of undeserved unmerited favor are spoken to us.

Being an heir of the God of Existence, now that is something you might want to attempt to grasp with your mind, as much as you can, the bigger we see God, the more we allow Him to flow through us.

As heirs, we inherit all the blessings of Abraham, including all the promises the Father made about Jesus. 2 Corinthians 1:20 says, "In Him, all promises are yes and amen."

Prayer

Father, I thank You that You adopted me and have made me Your own child. I thank You that You are a loving God. A God whose desire is good and blessing toward Your children, I thank You that I am not a slave to my former tasks master, but I am free to be a Child of God. I bless You and thank You that I am now of House Christ. I thank You that because of that, I am a co-heir of Your kingdom and blessings. I thank You for Your Word and Your love and the lengths that You went to graft us into Your family. I thank you that I am the apple of your eye. Amen.

Declaration

I am royalty, I am of house Christ, I am adopted, I am Loved.

-9-

I Am Anointed

"Now it is God who establishes both us and you in Christ.
He anointed us"
2 Corinthians 1:21 Berean Study Bible

I don't know about anyone else who is reading this book but, when I first became a believer, I used to think about the phrase of being anointed as something very vague and something that only a select few people have over their lives. I used to think it was the pastors of the church or the prophets who would visit the church once in a while, but I never thought of myself as anointed. I was never taught that I was anointed. As I have mentioned in every chapter, we who are in Jesus are everything that Jesus is.

Being anointed is simply being empowered. For me to think about being empowered, I visualize a specific pink bunny with a large battery in its back. This bunny keeps going and going always having power. We who are in Christ have an even better power source, the Holy Spirit. He was given to us and is the power source the gospel is talking about in 1 John 2:27, "And as for you, the anointing which you received from Him abides in you, and you have no need for anyone to teach you, but as His anointing teaches you about all things, and is true and is not a lie, and just as it has taught you, you abide in Him" New American Standard Bible.

To say that it's as simple as a battery is not the idea here. The real source is where the power comes from. The battery is just the housing for the power; our empowering comes from the Father who is the King of all authority, He, Himself has anointed us and has given us the power to walk in

His name. Like a signet ring in ancient days, the one who had the ring had all the authority that the one who anointed him has.

Now, what does it mean to anoint? You ever get out of the shower on a cold winter day and find yourself needing to moisturize your skin? Maybe you are one of those people who have never had that pleasure and have to put lotion on their bodies to protect themselves from the sun. When you are rubbing that lotion or moisturizer on yourself, that is what it means to anoint. When I am out buying a moisturizer; I look for the brand that works on my skin and the one I like the fragrance of the best. I would have to believe and imagine that even with my taste, it would pale in comparison to the scent that God's anointing leaves on me. This anointing empowers us to carry the fragrance of the king, the aromas of life, love, joy, peace, patience, kindness, goodness, and self-control, faithfulness, and gentleness.

What is the anointing for? There are multiple reasons for the anointing. When the Father anoints us, it is also for a purpose. He is our shepherd, and He "anoints my head with oil" Psalm 23. The reason that the shepherd anointed the head of the sheep with oil was to keep bugs from landing on the sheep and annoying them; some insects would even try to lay their eggs in the membranes of the sheep causing immense pain and even death in some cases. The shepherd would make this oil as a deterrent. Sheep, who were anointed, were cared for by their owner, and they were happy sheep.

When the Father anoints us, we are empowered to walk in His protection. We are also empowered to walk in His calling over our lives. In ancient times those who were anointed were called to do a specific task. Prophets were anointed; to be able to proclaim God's word. 1 Kings 19:16 "Then anoint Jehu grandson of Nimshi to be king of

Israel, and anoint Elisha son of Shaphat from the town of Abel-meholah to replace you as my prophet. New Living Translation Priests were anointed to carry out their duties of worship and sacrifice.; Exodus 40:13, says, "You shall put the holy garments on Aaron, and anoint him and consecrate him, that he may minister to Me as a priest. New King James Version. Kings were anointed so they could rule; 1 Samuel 16:13 says, "So Samuel took the horn of oil and anointed him in the presence of his brothers, and the Spirit of the LORD came powerfully on David from that day forward. Then Samuel set out and went to Ramah." Christian Standard Bible. Objects were anointed so that they could be set aside for holy use; Leviticus 8:10 "Also Moses took the anointing oil, and anointed the tabernacle and all that was in it, and consecrated them." (King James Version) and the sick were anointed, for healing; Mark 6:13 "and many demons they were casting out, and they were anointing with oil many infirm, and they were healing them." Young's Literal Translation.

Jesus is the anointed one of God. R.C. Sproul's "Jesus Christ, Anointed One", lays it out like this:

"The meaning of Christ is drawn from the Old Testament. God promised the ancient Israelites that a Messiah would come to deliver them from sin. The idea of the Messiah is carried over into the New Testament with the title Christ. The Greek word Christos, from which we get the English word Christ, is the translation of the Hebrew term Mashiach, which is the source for the English word Messiah. Mashiach, in turn, is related to the Hebrew verb masach, which means "to anoint." Therefore, when the New Testament speaks of Jesus Christ, it is saying "Jesus the Messiah," which literally means, "Jesus the Anointed One."

Yet who are we to claim also to be God's anointed? Can we refer to ourselves as anointed? Let's look at the scriptures, and we will find other people who did. 2 Chronicles 6:42 Solomon refers to himself as anointed. In 1 Chronicles 16:19-22, you will also find that God's people are described as "anointed ones" We who are in Christ are the anointed ones of God. You have been anointed vessels of God. You have been cleansed by the blood of Jesus and have been filled with the Holy Spirit. The Holy Spirit not only dwells in you, but He is also upon you in great power. He comes to bring an anointing of love, peace, and freedom. I have taught you these things that you will know who you are, and so that you would walk in the power that was given to you.

The very fact that you are anointed means that you don't have to do it by yourself. When you try with your own strength, you will surely come short. When you work with your own ability, you are at a disadvantage. Even people who say they are "self-made" would not have been able to do anything had it not been for the grace of God. You are anointed, there is a divine power enabling you to complete the task that is before you. With this empowerment, God is "able to do infinitely more than all we ask or imagine, according to His power that is as work within us" Ephesians 3:20 Berean Study Bible. When the task before you looks like it is something that you will not be able to overcome, remember at what Isaiah said: "the yoke shall be destroyed because of the anointing" Isaiah 10:27 King James Version. All of the things that would typically keep you from reaching the goal shall be destroyed. You are in Christ, and you are the anointed of God.

Prayer

Father, it is hard to find words to express the joy that I have knowing that I am by anointed You. I bless You because You have empowered me by The Holy Spirit. You have created me to walk in Your power and authority. Thank You that because of You, I am created to be a carrier of Your presence. You enable me to walk into the calling for my life. Because of the empowerment, I carry the fragrance of the Fruits of the Spirit. I thank You that You have made All of this is possible and it is all because I am in Christ. Amen.

Declaration

I am empowered, and the Holy Spirit is the proof.

-10-

I Am Chased

*"Surely your goodness and unfailing love will pursue me all
the days of my life, and I will live in the house
of the LORD forever."*
Psalm 23:6 New Living Translation

When I was a child, I used to play outside a
lot. I was outside so much that I had to be dragged
into the house by my ears. Wait, don't tell me that
you don't relate to that? Well, anyway, other than
our countless hours running around outside and
my memories of my Grandmother yelling for me to
come upstairs from her 2nd-floor window or my
mother telling me she would lock me out the house
if I weren't in before dark. One of my fondest times
was when we would play tag. It is a very basic
game, but it was one of the best games ever. There
would be one person who is "It" and the rest of the

people would run away while being chased by the person who is "It".

This simple game of chasing after something or someone didn't stop when we grew up a bit, but rather it manifested itself in different ways. We chase after new opportunities, new advancements, new headways, and further acknowledgment. We chase after new eateries, new companions, new forms of entertainment, and new innovations. We chase after love; we chase wealth and are always in the pursuit of something we think will make us happy. While we may love the chase, I believe what we love the most is the feeling of being chased. It is when we are pursued or sought after that we feel we are worth something. It is then that we don't feel like we have been overlooked or forgotten.

If our Father says, we are worth so much that He gave Jesus for us who are we to argue that fact? Our Father is the God of Truth, and there is no lie in Him. Everything that the Father tells us about Himself and ourselves is the truth. There is no lie that our Father won't tear down with His love. He will tear down the lies that we are told about Him, the lies that we are told about ourselves and the lies we tell ourselves.

Here is the truth... God is "It", you are not abandoned, you are not left alone, and you are not forgotten. He is chasing after you because you are worth it. He is in hot pursuit of you, and you might be imagining that He is out to get you so that He could punish you or to make your life boring, but there is nothing that could be further from the truth. The word chase is a simile for pursuing. In Hebrew, the word for pursue is radaph. Radaph means to chase, follow hard after, hunt, and pursue closely. Being chased by God is likened to the idea of an animal who is hunting their prey, they won't stop or give up, always chasing after them until they overcome them. He chases us in the pits of our lives. He chases us in the palaces of our lives just with the hopes of getting our attention. He is always chasing after us to overcome with the love He had for us from the beginning. That love culminated in the work of Christ on the Cross. I remember growing up and telling people "I love you this much" as I stretched my arms as wide as they could go, and it causes me to think that God is telling us the same exact thing as I envision Jesus' arms stretched out on the Cross just to show us His love for us.

God's lovingkindness pursues us always because we are in Christ. The Hebrew word for lovingkindness is hesed. The meaning of hesed is mercy, loyalty, forgiveness, faithfulness, covenantal love, undeserved love, steadfast love, never-ending love, and loyal love. This love goes above and beyond the call of duty. It is a love that is kind, good, and merciful. His love pins us down, and it's not a love that is suffocating but rather one that is freeing.

Need further convincing? The Word teaches us that He is not coming to take from our lives but rather to add to it. Look at what Jesus had to say in John 10:10, "The thief does not come except to steal, and to kill, and to destroy. I have come that they may have life, and that they may have it more abundantly." (New King James Version) The Father only adds to the life of those who are in Jesus. In fact, it is because we are in Jesus that the Lord's goodness and blessings can flow to us. Since our creation, it was our Father's will to be gracious to us, but due to the fall of man, the goodness that existed was blocked from flowing freely. He was not able to open the flood gates of Heaven towards us until Christ. Let us look at Isaiah 30:18, "Therefore the LORD longs to be gracious to you, And therefore He waits on high to have compassion on you. For the LORD is a God of justice; How blessed are all those who long for Him." (New American Standard Bible) God longed to be gracious to us, but he could not until Christ came and made way for the fullness of His goodness to be able to reach us righteously. Us being in Christ has positioned us to be the recipients of God's graciousness, and the pipe filled with God's goodness can now freely flow because of Christ.

To better understand the blessings that chase after us, let close out this chapter with the New International Version's rendition of Deuteronomy 28: 1-13. Here we find all of the blessings that come upon us because of Christ's perfect obedience. Take it all in; Tag, you're it. You are now caught by His blessings.

28 If you fully obey the Lord your God and carefully follow all his commands I give you today, the Lord your God will set you high above all the nations on earth. 2 All these blessings will come on you and accompany you if you obey the Lord your God:3 You will be blessed in the city and blessed in the country.4 The fruit of your womb will be blessed, and the crops of your land and the young of your livestock—the calves of your herds and the lambs of your flocks.5 Your basket and your kneading trough will be blessed.6 You will be blessed when you come in and blessed when you go out.7 The Lord will grant that the enemies who rise up against you will be defeated before you. They will come at you from one direction but flee from you in seven.8 The Lord will send a blessing on your barns and on everything you put your hand to. The Lord your God will bless you in the land he is giving you.9 The Lord will establish you as his holy people, as he promised you on oath, if you keep the commands of the Lord your God and walk in obedience to him. 10 Then all the peoples on earth will see that you are called by the name of the Lord, and they will fear you. 11 The Lord will grant you abundant prosperity—in the fruit of your womb, the young of your livestock and the crops of your ground—in the land he swore to your ancestors to give you.12 The Lord will open the heavens, the storehouse of his bounty, to send rain on your land in season and to bless all the work of your hands. You will lend to many nations but will borrow from none. 13 The Lord will make you the head, not the tail. If you pay attention to the commands of the Lord your God that I give you this day and carefully follow them, you will always be at the top, never at the bottom.

Prayer

Thank You, Father, that You chase us. Thank You that You did not give up on us. Thank You that You did not quit showering us with Your love. Thank You that You are the One who did not forget us or abandon us. We thank You, Father, that Your love continues to pursue us until You enamor us. We thank You that You chase us with Your goodness and mercy all of the days of our lives. Amen.

Declaration

I am chased.

I Am Beloved

"And suddenly a voice came from heaven, saying, "This is My beloved Son, in whom I am well pleased."
Matthew 3:17 NKJV

Captured by her gaze and beholding her as she was the only other being in the world. "I do," the groom proclaimed as he looked at his beautiful sparkling bride while trying to hold back the tears in his eyes. "You may now kiss your bride" said the Pastor, they kissed, and they were now married.

I've gone to many weddings throughout my life, and there isn't a wedding at which I didn't have fun. It is a celebration of love and of the joining of two people going forward to become one. I've been able to witness couples who have been together as long as I could remember, here's looking at you, Consuelo and Piro! I have even been engaged to get married before, but I could never wrap my mind around the idea that we are the bride of Christ and that He is our Husband. I am unsure if the reason I struggled to understand this was that I always related a bride with gender and social roles, but there was something about this idea that was just foreign to me. It wasn't until I received what I believe is a revelation from the Lord, that I was able to understand what He is talking about, that it finally became real to me.

It never dawned upon me that the word husband is the root word for husbandry. For those who don't know what husbandry is. It's merely the cultivation or production of plants or animals (thanks Merriam-Webster). One day, I'm not sure how it came about, the Lord allowed me to realize the picture He wanted me to see. To understand what He was trying to teach me, He likened the image of a husband to someone who does husbandry. A gardener, farmer, animal raiser or breeder. He already calls us the sheep of His flock, as He is our shepherd, you can find that in Psalm 23. It also got me thinking about the various times Jesus spoke about Himself being the vinedresser. One thought led me to another, and it got me to the place where I now understood that He is our Gardener, and we are His garden. A gardener prepares the soil, plants the seeds, waters, protects, prunes, cultivates, reaps, and more. He is the one who does all those things for His church, for His bride, for His garden. We are His garden, and because of that, we can trust in His protection, provision, correction, direction, and more.

This is something that God said He would do for us. In Hosea, He said He would betroth us to Him, bethroh us to Him in righteousness, justice, loving devotion, compassion, and faithfulness. (Hosea 2:19-10) The Cross is the altar at which the Son said: "I Do, I choose you!" It was there with five pointy objects that we were betrothed to our Gardener forever. The two nails in His hands, the spike keeping His feet bound to the base of the Cross, the nail used to place the notice that He is the king of the Jews above His head, and the spear that pierced His side is what God used to commit Himself to us forever. Isaiah 54:5 puts it this way, "For your husband is your Maker--the LORD of Hosts is His name--the Holy One of Israel is your Redeemer; He is called the God of all the earth. Berean Study Bible.

What else does it mean? Because I am Married to Christ, He calls me His beloved. "I am my beloved's, And my beloved is mine. He feeds his flock among the lilies". Song of Solomon 6:3 New King James Version. I am sure you would like to know what it means to be God's beloved? It means that God is well pleased with you; you are His delight, acceptable, and a sweet-smelling aroma to Him. Let us look at the scriptures. In

Matthew 3:17, we find the following "And a voice from heaven said, "This is my Son, whom I love; with him I am well pleased." New International Version. Here the Father was talking about the Son, and as we have covered several times since we are in the Son, what God says about Jesus, it is also true with us. We must understand and see ourselves as our Heavenly Father sees us. He sees us and is pleased with us because He sees Jesus' complete work. Whenever the Father looks at us, He sees Jesus, the one in whom He is well pleased.

Many people have the misconceptions that we must be doing things for God to be pleased with us. It is not our doing, but rather our belief. Not because of what I say or because of what I do but because I am in Christ, and Christ was the ultimate lover of God the Father. Because I am a lover of God, I am blessed with all the blessings of God. There were many times that I thought loving

God was doing something, but it is not. If we just rely on what we do, then we would be able to boast. It is by His grace that He is pleased with us. In Him, we find our worth and our identity.

Now am I saying go out and do crazy things in life because no matter what crazy thing you do, you don't have to worry because God is pleased with you? Allow me to be very clear that is not what I'm saying at all! What I am saying is this, believe Jesus and everything He did for us, and when we believe right, right living will be a by-product of our believing. The Fruit of the Spirit will continue to multiply in our lives when we listen to the correct voice. That is what solidifies the desires in us to want to make our Father proud of us. It is all about His righteousness and not our own. We need to understand that nothing we do or don't do can change the fact that the Father loves us and calls us His Beloved in Christ. You read that right NOTHING. Don't believe me, check It out for yourself.

> *5 Who will separate us from the love of [m]Christ? Will tribulation, or distress, or persecution, or famine, or nakedness, or peril, or sword? 36 Just as it is written, "For Your sake we are being put to death all day long; We were considered as sheep to be slaughtered."37 But in all these things we overwhelmingly conquer through Him who loved us. 38 For I am convinced that neither death, nor life, nor angels, nor principalities, nor things present, nor things to come, nor powers,39 nor height, nor depth, nor any other created thing, will be able to separate us from the love of God, which is in Christ Jesus our Lord. Romans 8:35-39 New American Standard Bible*

What does it say? "That I am convinced" Who is this that is writing this portion of God's word? Well, it would be none other than Paul, I know you have heard of him, right? The same Paul who cosigned to the death of the first martyr after Jesus. Yes, he just stood there holding the coats of the men who killed Stephen. The same Paul who states that he is the chief amongst sinners. This very same Paul, by the grace of God, has a meeting with the resurrected Jesus. This same Paul, who then went on to pen 2/3 of the New Testament. If he said that he was convinced, then who am I to argue with him? (not to mention that scripture is God's word) He stated that NOTHING could separate us from the love of God, let me repeat that because you must get that in your mind. Again, NOTHING! Not choice of clothing, music, denomination, political party, tattoos, bacon, or even yourself ... NOTHING!

OK, so now that we got that out of the way. Since nothing can separate us from God's love and we are His beloved, then God is well pleased. Not only is He well pleased with Jesus' complete work at the Cross, but also with us that we believe Him. For that is the work and will of God that we believe in His Son. Take a peek at what John 6:29 and 40 state respectively "Jesus answered and said to them, "This is the work of God, that you believe in Him whom He has sent." and "For this is the will of My Father, that everyone who beholds the Son and believes in Him will have eternal life, and I Myself will raise him up on the last day." New American Standard.

Our love for God will come naturally for us; it will be the overflow of what God is doing in our lives. When we realize and accept the fact that the Father loves us, our love for Him will continue to grow. Scripture says that "We love him, because he first loved us." 1 John 4:19 King James Version. God, Himself, calls me a lover of God. Romans 8:28, states that "God works all things for those who love God, to those called according to his purpose." We, believers, are the ones who are called according to the purpose of God, so we are those that love God.

Prayer

Father, I thank You that it was as the Cross that You decided the marriage should take place. I thank You that when you look at me, You see the precious blood of Jesus and because that is what You see, You are pleased with me. I thank You that You call me Your beloved. I thank You that You are my gardener. I thank You that I can walk in the freedom knowing that under the new covenant You are not angry with me, but rather You are pleased. I thank You that there is nothing that can change that, and I thank You that You have done it on our behalf. Amen.

Declaration

I am His Beloved

-12-

I Am Heard

*"I love the LORD because he hears my voice
and my prayer for mercy."*
Psalm 116:1 NLT

"MOM!!! MOM!!! Come quick!" I said one night when I was about 12 or 13. I woke up in the middle of the night; the room was dark; it was tranquil in the house as everyone was asleep. I didn't know what time it was. I could barely see since I didn't have my glasses on, yet I was able to see a blinking red light. Instantly my heart started pounding, and I was frozen from fear. I thought it was an alien or a demon or one of the many creatures my family said would come to get me if I misbehaved. I remember hiding my head under the covers and peeking again to see if the light was still there. Sweating and holding my breath, all I could think of at that moment was, "please; someone save me!" "MOM!! MOM!!" I cried out again, and my mother came rushing to see what the problem was. Her room was right next to mine, and I could hear her door swing open, then she stormed in the room, turned on the light, and was like, "what's wrong!?" Relieved because she heard me and came running, I started to tell her about the light only to realize that it was just the iron that was left plugged in and was flashing to indicate that it was in standby mode.

Why do I share this slightly embarrassing story? It's simple. I hoped to illustrate how good it feels when we cry out, and someone hears us. God doesn't only hear us when we are in distress; Genesis 16:11. "And the angel also said, "You are now pregnant and will give birth to a son. You are to name him Ishmael (which means 'God hears'), for the LORD has heard your cry of distress." New Living Translation. Instead, He always hears us in fact; He longs to hear from us. Ladies and gentlemen, if our parents hear us when we call out to them, how much more God? God hears us when we pray, and He loves when we speak with Him? What is prayer? In my opinion, prayer is merely (and I use the term honorably) conversing with God.

It is God's desire for us to know Him and have a relationship with Him. One of the best ways to have a relationship with someone is to build one via communication. What I love the most about prayer is that God can take it. I don't have to be fake with God; I could be real and honest because He can take it. In all reality, He knows it all anyway, so there should be no reason to try to hide things from Him. In the Garden of Eden, when man chose to listen to the wrong voice, there was a moment that they were scared. Genesis 3:10 gives us insight into what Adam said and felt. "So he said, "I heard Your voice in the garden, and I was afraid because I was naked; and I hid myself." King James Version. Adam was trying to hide from the God whom he had been accustomed to conversing with. You and I don't have to hide from God because we are no longer naked, we have been covered with Christ, and because of that, we can always approach Him.

Now, this isn't a chapter on all the things that can be written about prayer, there are millions of books about that, but I thought it to be vital to understand a little bit about it. Prayer can be inaudible and audible. In 1 Samuel 1, an account is written about the mother of Samuel, who was praying a silent prayer yet was heard by the LORD. David wrote in Psalm 116:1, "I love the LORD because he hears my voice and my prayer for mercy." David knew that God heard him. If you take a look at the Gospel of John 11:41-21, we read an account of one of Jesus' prayers, here you will find the following words "...And Jesus lifted up His eyes and said, "Father, I thank You that You have heard Me. And I know that You always hear Me..." Knowing that Jesus is always heard and knowing that we are in Jesus, this leads to a greater burden of proof that the Father always hears us also. Due to us being in Christ, we have access to the Father; we have God's ear. The Old Testament can further help us understand why we are heard because, after all, the Old Testament was a foreshadow of the things that were to come. In 2 Sam 24:18-24 & 1 Chronicles 21:18-28, we find David purchasing a place to build an altar "so that the prayers of the people could be heard," it is here that David purchased this land with silver and gold. Understanding why we are heard goes back to the blood of Jesus. It is His blood that has purchased for us a spot before the Throne of God, because of that, we can know that we are heard. The scripture states, "Let us then approach God's throne of grace with confidence (in His Blood), so that we may receive mercy and find grace to help us in our time of need." Hebrews 4:16 NIV. - Parenthesis mine. Being made righteous in Christ has given us access to the Father, and that access has paved the way for powerful prayers. James puts it this way. "...The prayer of a righteous person is powerful and effective." James 5:16b NIV

Prayer is communion with God, but to me, it is also an exercise of faith. I believe that God hears and answers prayer so, for me to pray to Him is me exercising my faith or putting it in action or working my faith. For "And without faith it is impossible to please Him, for he who comes to God must believe that He is and that He is a rewarder of those who seek Him." Hebrews 11:6 NASB. When we reach out to Jesus in prayer, we should believe that He hears and believe that He will answer. Otherwise, we wouldn't be praying, and to me, that is the prayer of faith.

Our faith causes us to be heard. In two different accounts in the Gospels, Jesus commended to two specific people about great faith. He praised a Roman Centurion and a Syrophoenician woman. Interestingly enough, both of those people were not Jews; therefore, they were not under the law. Both individuals were gentiles, yet their great faith was exalted above even the Jewish people who were in the vicinity. They were able to see that the grace of God, Jesus, had made Himself available to them, and they simply reached out to the available grace, believing that His grace was sufficient, fully able and fully willing.

Prayer

Father, first, I believe that You are, and that Is why I pray to You. I thank You that You consider me righteous because of the work of Christ, I thank You that you tell me that the prayers of the righteous are very effective. I thank You that You hear my prayers, and You answer them. I thank You that You purchased for us a place where our prayers are answered with the Blood of Christ. I thank You that You reveal Yourself as the Lord who Hears. I thank You that You have also placed me in the position to pray for others. Amen.

Declaration

I am someone who has God's ear, He hears me, and He answers my prayers.

Conclusion

It took me quite some time to write this book, and while it does not contain all that I had initially desired it to contain, I felt that it needed to be out there so that people could be blessed by the work I believe the Lord has given me to complete. I wrote these things so that you could know the truth. John 8:32 says, "Then you will know the truth, and the truth will set you free." The things that our Father says about us are in no way shape or form fully covered in this small book; after all, He wrote a 66 book love letter to us telling us all about Christ and who we are in Him. It is my hope that after reading this book, you see yourself in a better light because truth be told, you are the light of the world (Matthew 5:14).

During our journey through this book we have gone over ten different designations of who we are in Christ, and as I stated, there are plenty more. It is my prayer and hope that you indeed took to heart the things that you read during our journey together. Remember, it is not about who anyone else says you are; it is about who Your creator states you are. With all that said, I'll give you a bonus designation not counted in the original ten.

This designation is special to me because I believe all of the previous ones lead to or result in this one, freedom. Knowing who you are will lead you to immense freedom, and "if the Son sets you free, you are truly free" (John 8:36 NLT).

There is nothing that I truly desire more than freedom. Ask anyone who knows me; I value my time more than anything. Now that doesn't mean I don't like to lounge around and take in a good movie or a great book, of course, I do. But if you were to ask anyone they would tell you I love my freedom because I love to be able to do what I want when I want. I live in Buffalo, NY, and a large part of my family lives in the greater New York City area. As long as I could remember, I would be back and forth between the two locations. I wouldn't be able to do so had it not been for my freedom.

A perfect example of how much I loved my freedom came during the summer of 2017. I was working for a Fortune 15 company making really good money for the city that I live in, enough to where I could buy what I wanted in cash. I had no kids, and no real responsibilities other than myself. Yes I make sure those who are around be are well taken care of but other than that no real responsibilities to others. I had worked for this company for about four years, and while I made friends and connections that I believed would last a lifetime, something was missing. I was missing my freedom. So I up and quit.

I have always dreamed of being free to be a blessing to others. Free to come and go as I pleased. Free to serve when there was a need and more. I wanted to be in a place where I am free to be me, the real me, the me that God created me to be. I wanted to exist in a reality where I have no limits and no boundaries. I wanted to be free to be in the position to give without hesitation. Free to finance the Kingdom, teach people about the Word, free to eventually be the "Worlds #2 Dad" (Our Heavenly Father is #1). I want to be free to be there for my siblings and family, free to travel and go camping, go out to national parks, drive-in movies on summer nights, art museums, or just play the game. I want to be free to create memories for those I have the honor of influencing, and since I am a carrier of His presence, I want to be around others as much as possible. I want to be free to be a light to the world, salt to the earth, and a place of refuge. I want to be free to share God to the world in a practical manner, that they may see God even though they don't know what He looks like. Free to be a friend that sticks closer than a brother. Free to be a companion. Free to be a prayer warrior. Free to be a leader of men, a trainer of children, and a protector of women. Free to explore the world, to be love on display and love in action. I just long to be me!

I could go on and on about what freedom looks like to me, and I'm sure some of the people reading this were probably thinking to themselves one or two things. #1 "What is stopping you?" and #2 "I want to be free also." I have good news for you; we are FREE.

Looking at the main verse of this chapter, you will see that we are free. There are many other scriptures that further speak to our freedom. Romans 8:2 has this to say about our freedom, "For in Christ Jesus, the law of the Spirit of life has set you free from the law of sin and death." Being that we have been set free, we don't have to conform to the world and what it says about us or be directed by our fears. We are free to be exactly who God created us to be. He created us to be free to be His children. Romans 8:15 declares it this way, "For you did not receive a spirit of slavery that returns you to fear, but you received the Spirit of sonship, by whom we cry, "Abba! Father!" - To the slave He gives commands to the son He sets free."

God knows our likes and dislikes. He knows who He created us to be and what He created us for; His Glory. If He is so intimately involved with the smallest details in our lives, I assure you he created us to like and dislike certain things. He created us to be unique, and He purchased us to set us free. He is the God who is our Father and He pays attention to even the smallest details of our lives, I mean come on He even knows the number of hairs that we have on our heads as you will find in Matthew 10:30.The word states, "Before I formed you in the womb I knew you, And before you were born, I consecrated you; I have appointed you a prophet to the nations." (Jeremiah 1:5 NASB) Again, it states in the New Living Translation "You made all the delicate, inner parts of my body and knit me together in my mother's womb". Psalm 139:13. He knows us and knows He wanted us free.

It is my hope that you know more about yourself after reading this book. If you took this journey and you don't know God as your Father, but would like to, tell Him you accept what He says about you and what Christ did for you. If you did that, welcome to the family, you could now enjoy Him for the rest of eternity.